Grolier Enterprises, Inc. offers a varied selection of
both adult and children's book racks. For details on
ordering, please write: Grolier Enterprises, Inc.,
Sherman Turnpike, Danbury, CT 06816 Attn:
Premium Department

BOOK CLUB EDITION

WHAT DO SMURFS DO ALL DAY ?

WHAT DO SMURFS DO ALL DAY ?

by Peyo

BEGINNER BOOKS

A Division of Random House, Inc.

Copyright © 1983 by Peyo. All rights reserved under International and Pan-American Copyright Conventions. Published in the United States by Random House, Inc., New York, and simultaneously in Canada by Random House of Canada Limited, Toronto. *Library of Congress Cataloging in Publication Data:* Peyo. What do Smurfs do all day? SUMMARY: Relates in rhyme the myriad activities and occupations of Smurfs during a typical day. [1. Occupations—Fiction. 2. Stories in rhyme] I. Title. PZ8.3.P5Wh 1983 [E] 83-6070 ISBN: 0-394-86078-0 (trade); 0-394-96078-5 (lib. bdg.) Manufactured in the United States of America   C D   6 7 8 9
SMURF is a trademark of SEPP International S.A.

What do Smurfs do all day?

Papa Smurf says,
"Get out of bed!
It's time to get up,
you sleepyhead."

Smurfs brush their teeth
and wash their faces.
They scrub their necks
and other places.

Then they march
to breakfast
on fast feet . . .

...and eat and eat and eat.

And then, of course,

the Smurfs clean up.

They wash the dishes.

They mop the floors.

And then it's time
to go outdoors.

Every day
Smurfs like to play.

They like to hide
behind a bush.
They swing on swings.
They pull and push.

Smurfs love to pull.

They pull, pull, pull.

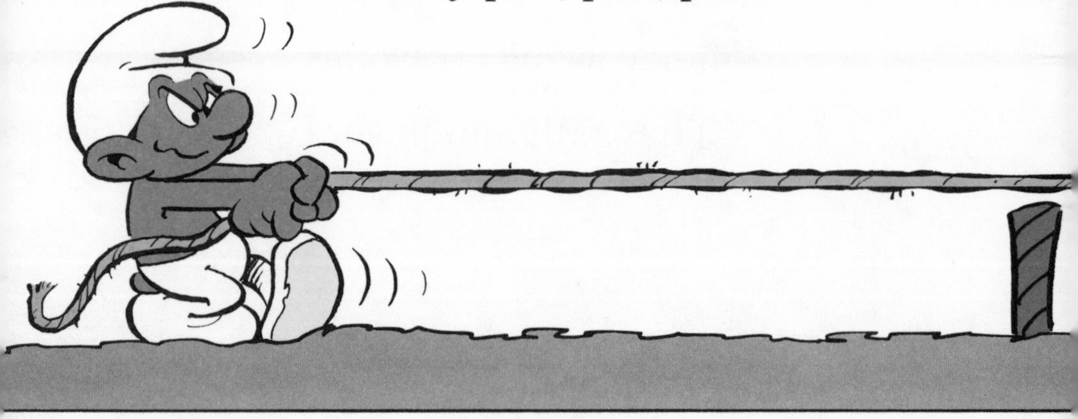

They dive in pools.

They splash about.

They swim and float

and then climb out.

Smurfs go to school.

They read.

They write.

Some spell quite well

and some not quite.

Then after school
they sing, they toot.

They clap their hands.
They howl and hoot.

They love to play.
And when they're through,
they work!
They all have jobs to do.

They stitch and sew,

they bake a cake.

They write a poem.

They hoe and rake.

They lift and lug.

They build and fix.

They scrape and paint.

They stir and mix.

What else do they do?

They snooze.

They sneeze.

And some play jokes.

They like to tease.

They laugh a lot.

Most days they're glad.

Sometimes they cry.

Sometimes they're sad.

Smurfs yell and shout!

Sometimes they mumble.

When they get mad

they grouch and grumble.

Some ride.

Some chase.

Some like to race.

Smurfs like to finish
in first place.

They throw and catch.

They hit the ball.

They ski and skate.

Sometimes they fall.

They run, they jump.

Smurfs love to tumble.

They pass and kick.

Sometimes they fumble.

They follow the leader.
They race about
until at last
they're all tired out.

And when their busy day is through,
they hop in bed, like me and you.

Then all night long,

what do they do...?

Smurfs dream their dreams.
They count their sheep.
They toss and turn
and snore . . . and sleep.